Learning About
Our Solar System

By
DEBBIE ROUTH

COPYRIGHT © 2004 Mark Twain Media, Inc.

ISBN 1-58037-281-3

Printing No. CD-404007

Mark Twain Media, Inc., Publishers
Distributed by Carson-Dellosa Publishing Company, Inc.

Table of Contents

one semester 16 weeks

Introduction

Hey, explorers, are you ready to tour the solar system in which we live? Our solar system is the sun and all of the objects that orbit it. It consists of one star (the sun), nine known planets with about 40 natural satellites circling them, millions of asteroids and meteoroids, and billions of comets. This book will be your guide to tour our neighbors in space. Your journey through the solar system will help you learn about its fascinating mysteries, including theories of origin, black holes and quasars, the galaxy in which we live (the Milky Way), and beyond. We live in a universe so vast that it is impossible to comprehend its size, shape, and scope. In fact, it was necessary to invent a system of measurement (the light-year) to make sense of it all. The knowledge we have gained about our space neighbors comes from various manned and un-manned space observatories. These probes orbit the earth and travel to the planets, providing us with new information about the nature of the celestial bodies and helping us gain an under-standing of the heavens above.

Explorers, you will use your scientific process skills as you discover many facts about your place within our solar system. The lessons and reinforcement sheets that follow the les-sons are written to engage the student explorer as well as inform. Most lessons will contain at least one higher-level thinking question. So, student explorers, put on those thinking caps and get ready to use your process skills as you embark on your journey through space ... **5, 4, 3, 2, 1, blast off!**

*Teacher Note: This book supports the National Science Education Standards and is designed to supplement your existing science curriculum or to be taught as a thematic unit on space. Each lesson opens with a manage-able amount of text for the student to read. The following pages are easy to read and contain exercises and illustrations that are interesting, varied, and plentiful. Simple definitions for terms are included to assist the student. The tone of this book is informal; a dialogue is established between the book and the student.

What Is the Solar System?

When you and your family travel on vacation, the world can seem very big. But to scientists who send probes into space or fly on space shuttles, these distances are actually very small. Earth is just one of a family of nine planets that circles our local star, the sun. The sun is at the center of our solar system. Although the most important objects in the solar system are the nine planets, it also includes smaller bodies. Most planets have natural satellites (moons) of their own. There are millions of "minor planets" called asteroids, meteoroids, billions of comets, and more. Even the space between bodies is not empty—comets leave tiny grains of dust and hot gases behind.

In order of distance from the sun, the planets are: Mercury, Venus, Earth, Mars, Jupiter, Saturn, Uranus, Neptune, and Pluto. The first four are the small, "rocky" inner planets. The next four are the giant "gaseous" outer planets. Pluto is an outer planet, even though it is small and rocky like the inner planets. Some scientists believe that Pluto is merely an asteroid. The inner and outer planets are separated by the asteroid belt, which contains billions of smaller rocks. Because the planets seemed to wander across the earth's sky, ancient Greeks called them *planets,* which comes from the Greek word meaning "wanderer." The planets **orbit** (move in a curved path) around the sun. The solar system is actually made up of the sun and everything that moves around it. It's a small part of a larger system known as the Milky Way galaxy; there are billions of galaxies beyond the Milky Way.

Distance in Space

Objects in space are very far apart. Scientists had to come up with a unit suitable for measuring such large distances in space. Scientists decided to use a unit called the "light-year" to try and make sense of the distances between objects in space. Light travels at a rate of 186,282 miles per second. A **light-year** is the distance light travels in one year, which is about 5.88 trillion miles. In space terms, our solar system is very small. It is only one "light-day" across. A light-day is the distance light travels in a day. In comparison, scientists have calculated the Milky Way galaxy to be 100,000 light-years across.

Origin

Scientists believe that the solar system formed from a spinning cloud of gas and dust called a **nebula**. Their theory is that gravity caused the nebula to shrink, or contract, to form the sun. After the sun formed, the leftover gas and dust in the nebula formed the other objects in our solar system. The sun, so big and extremely hot, is most of the mass (99%) of our solar system. Now that we know what the solar system is, let's continue our journey and get to know all of its other inhabitants.

Name: _____   Date: _____

What Is the Solar System?: Reinforcement Activity

To the student explorer: How many planets make up our solar system? Name them.

_____

_____

Analyze: Why do you think the planets are called wanderers? _____

_____

_____

Directions: Show what you have learned by answering the questions below.

1. What is a nebula? _____

_____

2. Which planets are the inner planets? _____

_____

3. Which planets are the outer planets? _____

_____

4. How are the inner and outer planets different? _____

_____

_____

Completion: Fill in the sentences below.

5. The _____ _____ separates the inner planets from the

    outer planets.

6. Scientists believe our solar system may have formed from a _____.

7. A planet's _____ is the curved path of the planet around the sun.

8. The sun is at the _____ of our solar system.

9. Objects in space are measured in a unit called a _____.

10. Our solar system includes the sun, nine planets, millions of minor planets called

    _____, and billions of _____.

What Is the Sun?

The sun is one of billions of stars in our part of the universe. That's right, explorers, I said the **sun** is a star. It is our local star; it is the center of our solar system. People used to believe that the earth was the center of the solar system and that the planets revolved around it. The sun is a gigantic, spinning ball of extremely hot gases, mostly hydrogen and helium. The sun is an average star in size, mass, and temperature; however, it is the largest object in our solar system. It is constantly in motion. It rotates once every 25 days, and it will revolve around our galaxy (the Milky Way) in about 230 million years. Because it is so huge, the sun's gravity exerts enough power to hold on to everything around it. It is the sun's gravity that keeps all of the planets **orbiting** (moving) around it in a regular orbital pathway. The sun is the only star close enough for us to study in detail.

The Sun's Energy

The sun is a huge solar furnace giving us just the right amount of light, heat, and energy, so that we can live comfortably here on Earth. It produces energy by nuclear reactions. The nucleus is the center of an atom. In a nuclear reaction, the nuclei of atoms are changed. Deep inside the sun, the temperature is so hot that the nuclei of hydrogen atoms combine, or fuse. This reaction, called **hydrogen fusion**, occurs when four hydrogen atoms fuse together to create one helium atom. Energy is released during the reaction from the leftover mass.

The Structure of the Sun

The sun is many layers of burning gas. It has two main parts: the core and the atmosphere. The **core** is deep within the sun's center. This is the hottest part of the sun where the sun's energy is created. Surrounding the core is the **radiative zone**. The temperatures in the radiative zone are highest at the core and coolest far away from the core. **Radiation** is the movement of energy from the hot core to cooler areas. The next area surrounding the core and radiative zone is the **convective zone**. The violent movements of gases in this layer carry energy to the sun's surface. The surface area of the sun is made up of three thin, **atmospheric layers**. The first layer is the **photosphere**, or light layer. It is the visible surface of the sun. The second layer is the **chromosphere**, or color sphere. It gives off a soft, red glow, usually seen during a solar eclipse. The last layer, the **corona**, gives a soft glow about half as bright as the moon and is usually seen during an eclipse. On the sun's surface are dark patches called **sunspots**. These areas are cooler than the areas around them and appear dark as a result. Sunspots move in groups in the same direction across the sun. Atoms of gases that carry electrically charged particles create them. The average life span of a sunspot is two weeks. Just remember, explorers, the bright light of the sun can be harmful to your eyes. You should never look directly at the sun.

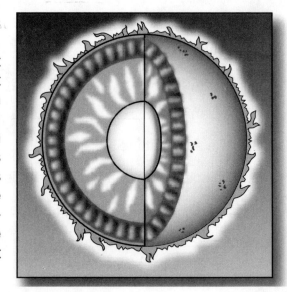

Name: _____   Date: _____

What Is the Sun?: Reinforcement Activity

To the student explorer: What kind of star is the sun? _____

_____

Analyze: Why does the sun appear to be so huge? _____

_____

Directions: Prove what you have learned so far about the sun by answering the questions below.

1. Of what is the sun mostly made? _____

2. What are the two main parts of the sun? _____

3. What is at the center of the sun? _____

4. What are the layers of the sun's atmosphere? _____

    _____

5. Which layers are only seen during a solar eclipse? _____

    _____

Directions: Solve the clues below. The first letter of each word has been provided.

6. A _____   One of the main parts of the sun

7. S _____   The center of our solar system

8. P _____   These orbit the sun due to gravity.

9. E _____   The corona is usually visible during this.

10. C _____   Hottest part of the sun

11. I _____   The sun is constantly _____ motion.

12. A _____   These are changed during a nuclear reaction.

13. L _____   The sun is the _____ object in our solar system.

14. S _____   Dark patches on the sun's surface

15. T _____   The sun has _____ thin, atmospheric layers.

16. A _____   The sun is an _____ -sized star.

17. R _____   Nuclear _____ produce energy.

The Inner Planets: Mercury, Extreme Desolation

The planets are divided into two groups based on size, location, and their composition. The first group, the **inner planets**, are the sun's closest neighbors. They include Mercury, Venus, Earth, and Mars. These planets have several things in common. They are small, dense planets made up of rocky material. They each have a central core of molten iron. The first stop on our journey through our solar system will be Mercury, the planet closest to the sun.

Mercury is a hot, heavy, lifeless planet with an enormous sun hanging in the black, airless sky. Mercury is slightly larger than our own moon. It is so close to the sun that astronomers cannot see the planet very well. It is only visible for a few days during each of its 88-day orbits of the sun. The Romans named Mercury after their swift messenger of the gods. Mercury travels fast around the sun. It completes one circuit of the sun (a Mercury year) in 88 earth-days. However, it **rotates** (spins) slowly on its axis. It takes 59 earth-days to make one complete rotation on its axis. The approximately 0-degree tilt of Mercury's axis causes the planet to revolve around the sun almost perfectly up and down. Much of what we have learned about Mercury is from the unmanned space probe *Mariner*. The *Mariner* probe made three passes near the planet in the early 1970s and sent back detailed information about the planet.

Life as we know it here on Earth could not exist on Mercury. Mercury's temperatures are too extreme. The temperature ranges from 410°C (842°F) during the day to -170°C (-292°F) at night. The planet has no atmosphere in which to hold the heat. Mercury has very little oxygen and no water. It has no natural satellites (moons).

In the 1990s, radar was used to study the surface of Mercury. We learned that the surface of Mercury is very similar to that of our moon. It is covered with craters created by meteorites (space debris) and has a few plains.

MERCURY FACTS

Planet closest to the sun; second-smallest planet

Diameter (equator)	4,878 km (3,050 miles)
Day	59 earth-days
Year	88 earth-days
Mass (relative to Earth)	0.055
Temperature (range)	410°C (842°F) day to -170C (-292F) night
Tilt of Axis	~0°
Number of Moons	0

Name: _____ Date: _____

Mercury, Extreme Desolation: Reinforcement Activity

To the student explorer: Do you recall what the two groups of planets are called?

_____

Analyze: Find the tilt of Mercury and describe how it revolves around the sun.

_____

_____

Directions: Answer the questions below.

1. Which planets are the inner planets? _____

    _____

2. What do the inner planets have in common? _____

    _____

    _____

3. What factors make life as we know it impossible on Mercury? _____

    _____

    _____

4. How is the surface of Mercury similar to the surface of Earth's moon? _____

    _____

Directions: Solve the clues below. The first letter of each word has been provided.

5. M _____ The sun's closest neighbor

6. E _____ The temperatures on Mercury

7. R _____ All inner planets are _____.

8. C _____ Made up of molten iron (two words)

9. U _____ The *Mariner* probe was _____.

10. R _____ Studied Mercury's surface

11. Y _____ 88 earth-days (three words)

The Inner Planets: Venus, the Hostile Furnace

The planet Venus is sometimes referred to as Earth's twin. It is similar to Earth in size, mass, and density. Venus is the second planet from the sun. It orbits between Mercury and Earth. It was named after the Roman goddess of love and beauty. However, Venus is a very hostile world. Its average temperature 465°C (869°F) is higher than the average of any other planet, making Venus a raging inferno. The gas (carbon dioxide) in its atmosphere and thick clouds of sulfuric acid make the surface features difficult to view. The atmospheric pressure is 90 times more crushing than Earth's air at sea level. Several early Soviet probes were crushed out of existence when they tried to land. The carbon dioxide gas, which is not breathable, traps the sun's heat and makes life (as we know it) impossible on Venus. The thick clouds that surround the planet reflect the sun's light, making Venus the brightest planet in the sky. It can even cast a shadow. Since the planet shines before sunrise and just after sunset, many people refer to it as the morning and evening star. Venus has a retrograde rotation. It spins slowly (243 earth-days) in the opposite direction from most of the other planets. It takes 225 earth-days to complete its orbit around the sun. Spacecraft visits have revealed that various surface features exist on Venus. Venus is oceanless like Mercury and has smooth rolling plains, stretches of highland plateaus, mountains, valleys, craters, and several active volcanoes. Like Mercury, Venus has no natural satellites.

VENUS FACTS

Second planet from the sun; sixth-largest planet, slightly smaller than Earth

Diameter (equator)	12,103 km (7,500 miles)
Day	243 earth-days
Year	225 earth-days
Mass (relative to earth)	0.81
Temperature (average)	465°C (869°F)
Tilt of Axis	2.6°
Number of Moons	0

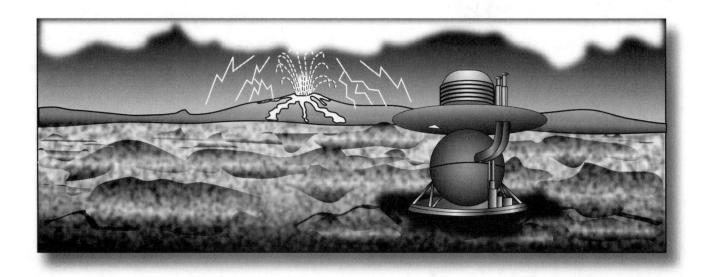

Name: _____   Date: _____

Venus, the Hostile Furnace: Reinforcement Activity

To the student explorer: Between which two planets does Venus orbit?

_____

Analyze: Why is Venus sometimes referred to as Earth's twin? _____

_____

_____

Directions: Answer the questions below.

1. What three factors make Venus a very hostile planet? _____

    _____

2. Why is Venus the brightest planet in the sky? _____

    _____

3. What gas in the atmosphere makes Venus so hot? _____

    _____

4. What happened when early spacecrafts tried to land on Venus? _____

    _____

5. Describe the surface features of Venus. _____

    _____

Directions: Solve the clues below. The first letter of each word has been provided.

6. V _____   _____ is sometimes referred to as Earth's twin.

7. E _____   Venus is sometimes called the _____ star.

8. N _____   Venus has no _____ satellites or moons.

9. U _____   Venus is _____ most planets; it rotates in the other direction.

10. S _____   Venus is the _____ planet from the sun.

The Inner Planets: Earth, the Planet on Which We Live

The next stop on our journey through space, explorers, is our home in space, Earth. The planet Earth is the third planet from the sun. It is the fifth-largest planet in our solar system. Earth is an active and lush planet with one natural satellite. As you can see from space, explorers, the earth and moon look like a double planet. The earth has an extraordinary blue color; seventy percent of the earth's surface is covered with water.

Earth is the only planet known to support life. Life as we know it occurs on Earth because of its favorable temperatures and atmosphere. We refer to the air that surrounds Earth as the **atmosphere**. Our atmosphere is mostly nitrogen (78%) and oxygen (21%). Earth has a very small percent of carbon dioxide and other gases. It has a magnetic bubble that protects us from the hostile environment of space. The moon, on the other hand, is a dead planet. The moon has no volcanoes and is airless and lifeless.

Earth rotates on its axis approximately every 24 hours. This gives us an equal amount of daytime and nighttime. A day is one complete rotation of the Earth around its axis. It takes the earth 365.25 days to revolve around the sun, creating one earth-year. Leap year gives February an extra day (once every four years) to make up for the extra one-fourth of a day in our year. Unlike Venus and Mercury, which circle the sun in a basically "upright" position, the earth does so at a 23.5° angle. The tilt of the earth is responsible for the seasons. When the sun is high in the sky, the sun's heat is more concentrated on the ground, creating summertime. Six months later, the planet is at the opposite side of its orbit. The sun is low in the sky, and the heat is more spread out, and it is winter. The Northern Hemisphere has winter in December and summer in June. The Southern Hemisphere is just the opposite.

The earth is composed of four layers. The first layer, the **inner core**, is a solid core of iron and nickel. The next layer, the **outer core**, is composed of melted iron and nickel. The third layer, the **mantle**, is a layer of rock that surrounds the outer core. The rock in the upper mantle is molten. The Earth's **crust** is the outermost, rocky layer of the earth. The surface of Earth is constantly changing as erosion and weathering occur. The heat currents rise from the center of our planet, the core, through the mantle, and slowly push the light "plates" of rocks around. This leads to earthquakes, volcanoes, new mountains, and continents. These surface changes are called **plate tectonics** and are unique to the planet Earth.

EARTH FACTS

Third planet from the sun; fifth-largest planet

Diameter (equator)	12,756 km (7,920 miles)
Day	23 hrs., 56 min.
Year	365.25 days
Mass (relative to Earth)	1.00
Temperature (average)	15°C (59°F)
Tilt of axis	23.5°
Number of Moons	1

Name: _____   Date: _____

Earth, the Planet on Which We Live: Reinforcement Activity

To the student explorer: What is responsible for the earth supporting life as we know it?

_____

_____

Analyze: What gives the earth its extraordinary blue color? _____

_____

Directions: Answer the questions below.

1. What provides us with an equal amount of day and night? _____

    _____

2. Which gas is most abundant in our atmosphere? _____

3. Why is the moon a dead planet? _____

    _____

4. The earth is composed of four layers.
    Identify each layer in the diagram.

    A. _____

    B. _____

    C. _____

    D. _____

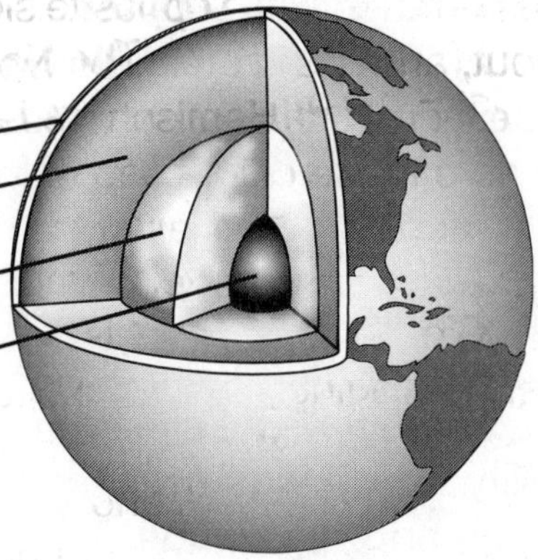

Directions: Solve the clues below. The first letter of each word has been provided.

5. E _____   The _____ is the third planet from the sun.

6. A _____   The _____ is the air that surrounds the earth.

7. R _____   Earth _____ on its axis every 24 hours.

8. T _____   The _____ of the earth is responsible for the seasons.

9. H _____   _____ currents rise from the center of our planet and cause earthquakes and volcanoes.

What Is Earth's Natural Satellite?

The Moon—Earth's Companion

The moon is the Earth's only natural satellite. Most planets with moons have more than one orbiting them. The earth and its moon travel together around the sun. The moon also orbits Earth. During the orbit, when the moon is farthest from Earth, it is at its **apogee**. When the moon is closest to the earth, the moon is at its **perigee**. The change in distance from the earth to the moon has an effect on Earth's tides and other things. The effect on tides is greatest when the earth, moon, and sun are aligned. The moon has less mass than the earth; therefore, the gravity on Earth's surface is six times greater than the gravity on the moon. The moon's weaker gravity means that you can jump much higher on the moon than you can on Earth. The first human to walk on the moon was Neil Armstrong. He and astronaut Edwin "Buzz" Aldrin found movement on the moon to be awkward because of its weak gravitational pull. The moon takes just over 27 days to complete one orbit of Earth. It rotates on its axis in about the same amount of time. Since its revolution and rotation periods are approximately the same, we can only see one side of the moon. Nearly one-half of the moon is always hidden from view.

Origin

The current belief suggests that the moon formed at about the same time as the earth. The earth collided with another object, and the core of the body that hit our planet became part of the moon. The lighter material began orbiting Earth and collected to form the moon. The word *moon* comes from the Greek word *lunar*, which means "month."

Surface Features

There are three main types of features found on the moon's surface. The dark areas, **maria** (plural for *mare*), are flat plains. Early astronomers thought that these areas were bodies of water. *Maria* is a Latin term that means "seas." The first astronauts landed in the Sea of Tranquillity, which was not a sea but a large, broad, flat plain instead. The light areas are **mountains and highlands**. The third surface feature is its many **craters**. The moon has no atmosphere or liquid water. The temperatures can range from over 100°C to -160°C (212°F to -256°F). Astronauts must wear protective space suits to survive on the moon.

What Is Earth's Natural Satellite? (cont.)

Phases of the Moon

The changing appearance of the shape of the moon is called its **phases**. It takes 29.5 days to go through all of the moon's phases. The positions of the sun, the moon, and the earth determine the phase. The moon appears to shine, because it reflects the light of the sun. The moon's appearance changes because of the way it reflects light from the sun. As it revolves, we see different amounts of the moon's surface. To find the dates of the moon's phases, check a newspaper, calendar, or almanac.

There are eight phases of the moon. In the first phase, the **new moon**, the moon's surface is not visible from Earth. As the moon revolves, the **new** or **waxing crescent** phase appears on the eastern edge. In the third phase, the **first quarter**, the right half of the moon is visible. During the fourth phase, the **waxing gibbous** phase, more than one-half of the right side of the moon is visible. Next, the **full moon** phase appears. After the full moon, we see a **waning gibbous** moon, where more than one-half of the left side of the moon is visible. During the **last quarter**, the left half of the moon is visible. Lastly, during the **waning crescent**, only the western edge can be seen. As the moon revolves around the earth, a small part becomes visible. As the visible part increases, the moon is said to be **waxing**. After the full moon, the moon enters the waning phases. As less and less of the surface is visible, the moon is said to be **waning**.

The boxes represent the view of the moon from Earth.

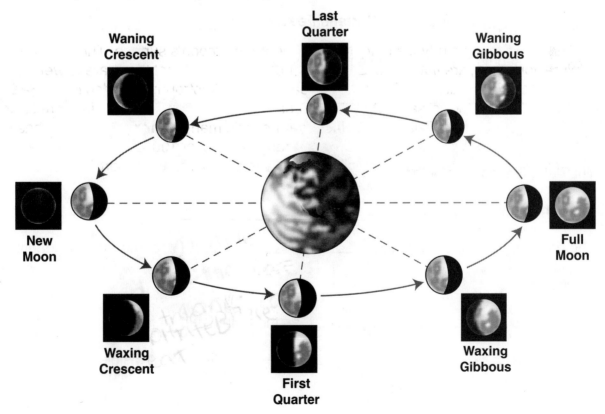

13

Name: _____ Date: _____

What Is Earth's Natural Satellite?: Reinforcement Activity

To the student explorer: Why are you able to jump higher on the moon than you can here on Earth?

_____

_____

_____

Analyze: Why do astronauts need to wear protective suits on the moon?

_____

_____

_____

Directions: Complete each sentence below.

1. The moon _____ on its axis.

2. The earth and moon travel together around the _____.

3. The moon seems to shine because it reflects _____.

4. _____ _____ was the first person to walk

    on the moon.

5. The dark, flat features of the moon are called _____.

6. The light areas of the moon are _____ and highlands.

7. The changing appearance of the _____ of the moon is identified

    by phases.

8. The moon is _____ as the visible part increases.

9. The moon is _____ as less and less of it is visible.

Name: _____ Date: _____

Earth's Natural Satellite: Moon Phases Activity

To the student explorer: Shade the circles below and label each circle to show the moon's appearance from Earth during each of the eight phases, beginning with the new moon phase.

THE PHASES OF THE MOON

1. _____

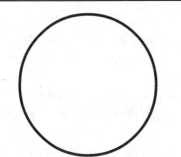

2. _____

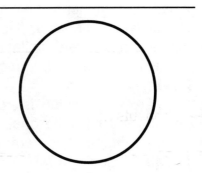

3. _____

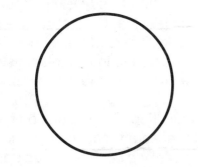

4. _____

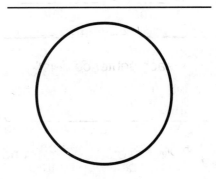

5. _____

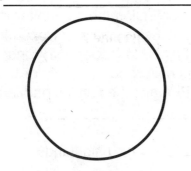

6. _____

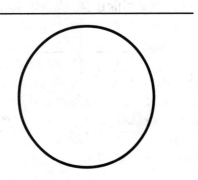

7. _____

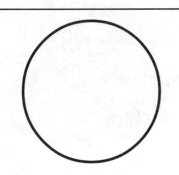

8. _____

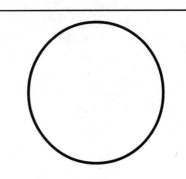

The Inner Planets: Mars, the Red Dust Bowl Planet

Mars is the fourth planet from the sun and the last of the inner planets. Mars is named for the Roman mythological god of war. No other planet has captured the imagination of people more than Mars. It is sometimes referred to as the "red planet" because of its reddish-orange surface color. At times, Mars appears in Earth's sky like a bright red star. Mars is not hidden by the sun's glare like Mercury or covered by thick clouds like Venus. Mars is relatively close to Earth. Mars is about half the diameter of the planet Earth, but it shares several similarities. The length of day is about the same on Mars as it is on Earth. Its rate of rotation is 24 hours and 37 minutes. Mars has longer seasons very similar to Earth's seasons because of a similar tilt on its axis. The air pressure is also about the same on Mars as it is on Earth. Mars' orbit period around the sun is 687 days.

Except for the polar ice caps, Mars is a dry planet. Some scientists believe that water is frozen in the polar ice caps and may have once been plentiful on the planet. Mars can be colder than Antarctica during the winter and as warm as a spring day in the United States. The average temperature on Mars is -50°C (-58°F). The atmosphere is thin and composed mostly of carbon dioxide. Mars can have winds of up to 100 km/h, creating severe dust storms that cover the planet. Mars has two small natural satellites (moons), Phobos (fear) and Deimos (panic). The moons were named after companions of the mythological war god Mars. Mars' surface has many craters caused by meteorites and is covered with loose rocks. There are giant ridges as a result of volcanic activity, as well as huge canyons. The largest volcano in the solar system, Olympus Mons, is found on Mars. Mars' surface resembles the surface of the moon more so than the surface of Earth.

Scientists were very excited by what appeared to be many dried-up riverbeds on Mars. This set the scene for the search for life on Mars. The *Viking* spacecraft reached Mars in the 1970s and sent back the first close-up pictures of the planet. Two *Viking* landers picked up soil samples and analyzed them in a small laboratory on board. All experiments conducted on the soil samples showed no signs of life. However, scientists are continuing the search for life on Mars. They believe there may be microscopic life forms locked inside rocks or frozen in the polar ice caps. In January 2004, the unmanned Mars rovers *Spirit* and *Opportunity* landed on Mars and began moving about the planet, taking pictures and collecting samples for testing. Plans for a manned expedition to Mars are being developed. Perhaps the first life on Mars will be humans; perhaps it will be you!

MARS FACTS

Fourth planet from the sun; seventh-largest planet

Diameter (equator)	6,794 km (4,220 miles)
Day	24 hrs., 37 min.
Year	687 earth-days
Mass (relative to Earth)	0.11
Temperature (average)	-50°C (-58°F)
Tilt of Axis	25°
Number of Moons	2

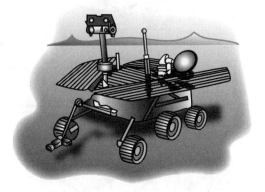

Name: _____ Date: _____

Mars, the Red Dust Bowl Planet: Reinforcement Activity

To the student explorer: Do you think the "red dust bowl planet" is an appropriate name for Mars? Why or why not?

_____

_____

Analyze: Why do you think we know so much more about this planet than the other planets in our solar system?

_____

_____

Directions: Answer the questions below.

1. If Mars once had water in its dried-up riverbeds, what might have happened to it?

   _____

   _____

2. How are Mars and Earth similar? _____

   _____

3. Could you live on Mars? How? _____

   _____

   _____

4. Where do scientists believe life forms may be on Mars? _____

   _____

Directions: Solve the clues below. The first letter of each word has been provided.

5. M _____ _____ is the fourth planet from the sun.

6. A _____ Mars can be colder than _____ in the winter.

7. R _____ Mars is sometimes called the _____ planet.

8. S _____ Mars' _____ has many craters and loose rocks.

17

What Are Minor Planets?

Asteroids and the Asteroid Belt

Between Mars and Jupiter lies a 300-million-mile gap called the **asteroid belt**. This gap contains leftover debris from the formation of our solar system. The debris field contains thousands of asteroids and chunks of rock and metals that orbit the sun. These pieces of rock, metal, and combinations of rock and metal are irregular in shape and vary in size; they are called **asteroids**. The largest asteroids measure a few hundred miles in diameter. Most are smaller and look like tumbling chunks of rock. Asteroids are sometimes referred to as "minor planets" or "planetoids." So as you can see, explorers, the nine planets and their moons are not the only bodies in our solar system. Some scientists believe that the powerful gravity of Jupiter may have prevented the debris in the asteroid belt from forming into a planet during the early history of our solar system. Others believe that the asteroids are the remains of planets that exploded a long time ago. Most asteroids orbit the sun in the asteroid belt located between Mars and Jupiter. However, asteroids have been identified in other areas of the solar system.

Meteoroids and Meteorites

Asteroids have been known to collide with other objects in space. Small pieces of both objects break off, forming what are known as **meteoroids**. Most of these small pieces are smaller than a grain of sand. If a meteoroid enters a planet's atmosphere, friction causes all or part of the meteoroid to burn. A bright light that streaks across the sky is a meteoroid that has entered Earth's atmosphere. Meteoroids that reach the planet's surface and actually land on Earth are called **meteorites**. Meteorites create craters upon impact with the surface. The best place to look for meteorites today is in Antarctica. However, most meteorites fall into the sea.

Meteors and Meteor Showers

Explorers, have you ever seen a shooting star? This bright streak of light that you saw is actually a **meteor**. As we have already learned, meteors are caused by meteoroids when they enter the Earth's atmosphere; friction heats the rock and creates a tail of hot gas. There are two types of meteors. One type of meteor, **sporadic meteor**, is a meteor that can appear at any time. Meteor displays where hundreds of meteors are seen at night during certain times of the year are called **meteor showers**. The meteoroids that fall in meteor showers are tiny, dust-sized particles from comets. This occurs when a comet's orbit takes it close to the sun. The sun melts some of the ice and releases trapped dust particles. As Earth passes through the dust left by a passing comet, the dust burns up in the atmosphere, and a meteor shower is produced. Meteor showers are predictable in that they occur at certain points in Earth's orbit; however, they vary in radiance. Astronomers believe millions of meteors come into Earth's atmosphere every day. Only a few move within 30 miles of Earth. Because they are so small, only the size of a grain of sand, most of them disintegrate from the heat and friction created by Earth's atmosphere.

Name: _____ Date: _____

What Are Minor Planets?: Reinforcement Activity

To the student explorer: Where is the asteroid belt located? _____

_____

Analyze: Why do you think asteroids are sometimes called minor planets? _____

_____

_____

Directions: Answer the following questions.

1. What are asteroids? _____

   _____

2. Where are most asteroids located? _____

   _____

3. What are meteoroids? _____

   _____

   _____

4. What are meteors? _____

   _____

   _____

5. Is "shooting star" an appropriate name? Why or why not? _____

   _____

6. Identify and explain the two types of meteors. _____

   _____

   _____

7. What is a meteorite? _____

   _____

8. Why do meteoroids usually disintegrate rather than fall to the earth? _____

   _____

   _____

The Outer Planets: Jupiter, the Gas Giant

All aboard, explorers! It's now time to journey to the outer planets. Thanks to the missions of the *Voyager* and *Galileo* space probes, we have learned a great deal of new information about the distant planets in our solar system. The outer planets include four huge, gaseous planets: Jupiter, Saturn, Uranus, and Neptune, plus the tiny planet of Pluto. We will continue our journey by visiting the planets in the order of their distance from the sun. Our first stop will be the huge planet of Jupiter.

Jupiter is the fifth planet from the sun and the largest known planet in our solar system. Jupiter was named after the king of the Roman gods. Over one thousand Earths could fit inside Jupiter. Because of its size, Jupiter can be seen without using a telescope. Jupiter has an atmosphere composed mostly of hydrogen and helium. Scientists believe that the hydrogen and helium gradually changed into liquid hydrogen, forming an ocean of liquid hydrogen, which covered the planet. Below the liquid layer is a solid rocky core. This means that the planet changes from outside to inside from a gas, to a liquid, to a solid. The pressure and temperature make the solid core different from any rock on Earth. Jupiter's rotation is very rapid; it spins once approximately every ten hours. This rotation rate causes colorful belts of clouds on the planet that are constantly changing. They range from red or orange to brown to white. The upper atmosphere is very stormy. One constant sight is the Great Red Spot—a huge storm. This swirling oval storm is similar to a cyclone. It is large enough to see from Earth by telescope. Scientists believe steam and ammonia rising from the atmosphere beneath Jupiter's clouds probably cause it. Jupiter's revolution is at a much slower rate. It takes the planet almost 12 earth-years to circle the sun. Jupiter is a very cold planet with at least 16 satellites or moons. Scientists were surprised to learn that two thin, faint rings circle Jupiter.

JUPITER FACTS

Fifth planet from the sun; the largest planet

Diameter (equator)	142,796 km (88,700 miles)
Day	9 hrs., 55 min.
Year	11.86 earth-years
Mass (relative to Earth)	318
Temperature (average)	-150°C (-302°F)
Tilt of Axis	3°
Number of Moons	16
Number of Rings	2

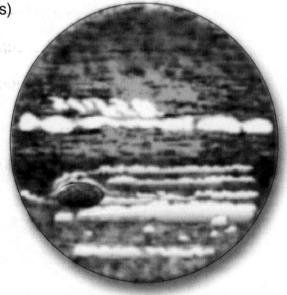

Name: _____   Date: _____

Jupiter, the Gas Giant: Reinforcement Activity

To the student explorer: How would you describe Jupiter? _____

_____

_____

Analyze: Do you think Jupiter is an appropriate name for this planet? Why or why not?

_____

_____

Directions: Answer the following questions.

1. What is the Great Red Spot? What causes it? _____

    _____

    _____

2. What two gases make up most of Jupiter? _____

    _____

3. Compare Jupiter's rates of rotation and revolution to Earth's rates.

    _____

Directions: Solve the clues below. The first letter of each word has been provided.

4. J _____ _____ is the fifth planet in our solar system.

5. U _____ Jupiter and _____ are both outer planets.

6. P _____ Jupiter is the largest known _____.

7. I _____ The outer planets _____ four large planets and one tiny planet.

8. T _____ Jupiter is large enough to be seen without a _____.

9. E _____ One year on Jupiter is equal to twelve _____ -years.

10. R _____ Jupiter's rotation is very _____ and causes colorful belts of clouds.

The Outer Planets: Saturn, the Ringed Planet

Saturn is the sixth planet from the sun and the second-largest planet in our solar system. Like Jupiter, Saturn is a gas giant made up of mostly hydrogen and helium. It is twice as far from Earth as Jupiter and often appears as a dim point of light in our night sky. It has an upper atmosphere containing bands of clouds moving around the planet. The clouds appear soft and creamy in color. There are no giant storms like Jupiter's Great Red Spot. Saturn also appears to possess a layer of liquid hydrogen and a rocky core. In spite of its enormous size, it has the lowest density. Its density is so low that if you could find a body of water large enough, the planet would actually float in water. In other words, Saturn's density is less than that of water. Its most distinctive feature, of course, is its rings. Saturn's rings can easily be seen from Earth with the use of even the least powerful of telescopes.

Rings and Moons

There are several main rings with thousands of thin ringlets orbiting inside each of Saturn's main rings. They are not solid bands but rather ice, rocks, and particles of dust that orbit the planet. This makes Saturn's ring system the most complex of all the gaseous outer planets. Rings aren't the only things that orbit Saturn. Scientists believe there may be as many as 30 moons orbiting this planet. The largest moon is Titan; it is larger than the planet Mercury. Titan's surface is covered with thick clouds, making it difficult for scientists to see its surface features. The moons orbit Saturn as it travels around the sun. It takes about 29.5 earth-years to complete one revolution, or Saturn year. Its rotation, on the other hand, is very swift; it completes one rotation in approximately 10.5 hours.

SATURN FACTS

Sixth planet from the sun; second-largest planet

Diameter (equator)	120,000 km (74,500 miles)
Day	10 hrs., 40 min.
Year	29.5 earth-years
Mass (relative to Earth)	95
Temperature (average)	-180°C
Tilt of axis	27°
Number of Moons	30
Number of Rings	Thousands

Name: _____   Date: _____

Saturn, the Ringed Planet: Reinforcement Activity

To the student explorer: How would you describe Saturn? _____
_____
_____

Analyze: Can you identify three similarities between Saturn and Jupiter? _____
_____
_____

Directions: Answer the following questions.

1. Why is it that this giant planet could float in water? _____
_____

2. Can you describe Saturn's ring system? _____
_____
_____

3. What has made studying Titan difficult? _____
_____
_____

Directions: Solve the clues below. The first letter of each word has been provided.

4. S _____   Saturn is the _____ planet in our solar system.

5. A _____   Saturn is _____ gas giant.

6. T _____   Saturn is _____ as far from Earth as Jupiter.

7. U _____   Saturn's rings can be seen with the _____ of a telescope.

8. R _____   Saturn's _____ are made up of ice, rocks, and particles of dust that orbit the planet.

9. N _____   The _____ of moons orbiting Saturn is higher than that of other planets.

The Outer Planets: Uranus and Neptune, the Pulling Planets

URANUS

All of the planets we have visited so far shine brightly in the night sky and have been known since early times; even their names are from ancient Roman gods. Uranus is the seventh planet from the sun and the third largest. It was named for the Greek god of the sky. Uranus was not discovered until 1781 and was the first planet to be discovered by a telescope. We knew very little about Uranus prior to the *Voyager 2* space probe mission in 1986. The *Voyager 2* sent back many images and revealed several interesting characteristics.

Uranus is a gas giant, but it is only half the size of Saturn. Uranus is made up of mostly hydrogen and helium like the other gaseous planets. The blue-green color of the clouds indicates that the atmosphere contains methane gas as well. Some scientists believe that the planet may have collided with another body early in its history, making the planet tip over onto its side. This horizontal axis and appearance of lying on its side is one of the interesting characteristics about Uranus. The other planets appear to move upright in their orbits. We have not been able to learn much about the surface features of Uranus. This bluish-green planet spins very fast and has a strong magnetic field. Its rotation is complete in about 17 hours. Its orbit around the sun takes about 84 earth-years. It also appears to have a faint ring about it, which is actually 11 rings made up of rocky chunks. Scientists have also observed 17 moons orbiting Uranus. The planet seems to be unable to hold its normal position in orbit. Scientists speculate that the planet changed its usual position because of the gravitational pull of an undiscovered planet.

NEPTUNE

It was another 65 years after the discovery of Uranus before another planet was identified in our solar system. Scientists suspected that an eighth planet existed because of the behavior of Uranus as it orbited the sun. They thought that the gravitational attraction of another planet was pulling Uranus off course. Calculations of the position of the unknown planet orbiting Uranus led to the discovery of Neptune.

Neptune is the eighth planet from the sun. It was named for the Roman god of the sea. It is similar in size to Uranus. Like the other gaseous planets, it is mostly made up of hydrogen and helium. Like Uranus, it has a bluish-green color, indicating that methane gas is also present. Neptune rotates in about 16 hours, but its atmosphere moves more slowly. It may take the clouds around the planet an additional two hours to complete their orbit. Neptune has dark-colored storms in its atmosphere similar to Jupiter's Great Red Spot. This huge oval storm cloud is about the size of Earth. The area seems to disappear, indicating that the atmosphere on Neptune is active and changes rapidly. Neptune is considered to be the windiest planet in our solar system. Its orbit around the sun takes about 165 earth-years. Neptune is thought to have a layer of liquid water, methane, and ammonia that might change to solid ice. It is believed that Neptune has a rocky core. Neptune has eight moons and four rings of dust particles surrounding it.

URANUS FACTS
Seventh planet from the sun; third-largest planet

Diameter (equator)	50,800 km (31,500 miles)
Day	17 hrs., 14 min.
Year	84 earth-years
Mass (relative to Earth)	15
Temperature (average)	-210°C
Tilt of axis	97.9°
Number of Moons	17
Number of Rings	11

NEPTUNE FACTS
Eighth planet from the sun; fourth-largest planet

Diameter (equator)	48,600 km (30,200 miles)
Day	16–18 hrs.
Year	165 earth-years
Mass (relative to Earth)	17
Temperature (average)	-220°C
Tilt of axis	28.8°
Number of Moons	8
Number of Rings	4

Name: _____ Date: _____

Uranus and Neptune: Reinforcement Activity

To the student explorer: How are Uranus and Neptune similar? _____

_____

Analyze: What do you think is the most unusual feature of Uranus? _____

_____

Directions: Answer the following questions.

1. What did scientists believe to be the reason Uranus could not hold its position in orbit?

   _____

2. What do the storms on Neptune indicate? _____

   _____

Directions: Solve the clues below. The first letter of each word has been provided.

3. U _____ The seventh planet is _____.

4. R _____ Uranus is another _____ planet with 17 moons orbiting it.

5. A _____ The _____ of Uranus is horizontal.

6. N _____ We did _____ learn much about Uranus until the *Voyager 2* mission.

7. U _____ Uranus has an _____ tilt.

8. S _____ Uranus spins fast and has a _____ magnetic field.

_ _

9. N _____ Neptune was _____ after the Roman god of the sea.

10. E _____ Neptune is planet number _____ from the sun.

11. P _____ Scientists _____ that an unknown planet existed because of the behavior of Uranus.

12. T _____ The _____ led to the discovery of these distant pulling planets.

13. U _____ The gravitational force of Neptune was pulling _____ off course.

14. N _____ _____ has dark-colored storms similar to Jupiter's Great Red Spot.

15. E _____ Neptune has _____ moons and four rings.

The Outer Planets: Pluto, the Ninth and Smallest Planet

Pluto is the smallest of all of the planets in our solar system. It is vastly different from the other outer planets. Pluto has a diameter of only 2,400 km (1,500 miles), which makes it smaller than Earth's moon. It was discovered in 1930, after decades of a deliberate search for an object that was thought to have an effect on the paths of Uranus and Neptune. Something seemed to be disturbing the orbits of both of these planets. We now know Pluto is far too small to have any effect on them at all. Could there possibly be another more distant, undiscovered tenth planet? For now, Pluto and its moon Charon mark the frontier of our solar system.

Pluto was named after the Roman god of the dead. It is the farthest planet from the sun, but its unusually tilted orbit occasionally brings it inside the orbit of Neptune. Pluto's orbit is lopsided and steeply tilted. It remains inside Neptune's orbit for 20 years of its 248-year orbit. Its rotation is completed in six earth-days. Because Pluto is so far away, we know little about it. The Hubble Space Telescope gave astronomers their first good look at Pluto and Charon as distinct objects. The planet appears as a very tiny point of light when using even the most powerful of telescopes. We have learned that it has only one moon, Charon, which is half the size of Pluto. Some scientists consider them to be a double planet. Other scientists question whether Pluto and Charon are members of the vast icy comets of the Kuiper Belt.

Pluto is surrounded by a very thin atmosphere and is the coldest planet in our solar system. Pluto is an icy planet with a rocky core and has methane ice on its surface. Until the planet is visited by a space probe, much about Pluto will probably remain a mystery.

This is the last planet on our journey through the solar system. Next, let's see what we can discover about our home galaxy, the Milky Way.

PLUTO FACTS

Ninth planet from the sun; the smallest planet

Diameter	2,400 km (1,500 miles)
Day	6 days, 9 hours
Year	248 earth-years
Mass (relative to Earth)	0.002
Temperature (average)	-230°C
Tilt of Axis	98.8°
Moons	1

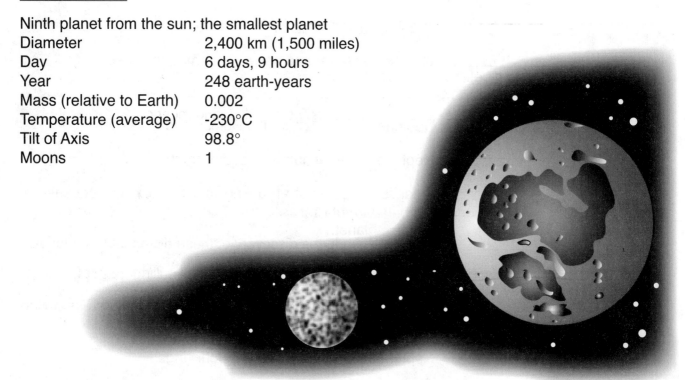

Name: _____ Date: _____

Pluto, The Ninth and Smallest Planet: Reinforcement Activity

To the student explorer: How would you describe the planet of Pluto? _____

_____

_____

Analyze: Why do scientists say Pluto is *usually* the ninth planet? _____

_____

_____

Directions: Since we know so little about Pluto, let's imagine that you are a news journalist and a scientist has just discovered a tenth planet. What would be five interview questions you would ask the scientist about the discovery? (Hint: Remember the 5 *W*s!)

1. _____

2. _____

3. _____

4. _____

5. _____

Directions: Solve the clues below. The first letter of each word has been provided.

6. P _____   _____ is the smallest and most distant planet.

7. L _____   The planet appears as a tiny point of _____ even with powerful telescopes.

8. U _____   Some scientists wonder if there is a tenth _____ planet.

9. T _____   Pluto's orbit is lopsided and steeply _____.

10. O _____   The tilt of Pluto's _____ occasionally brings it inside Neptune's orbit.

What Is a Comet?—A "Dirty Snowball"

Structure of Comets

Like the planets and the asteroids, comets are also members of our solar system. The appearance of a comet near Earth is a spectacular sight. These small members of our solar system are actually ice, rock, frozen gas, and dust. They are sometimes described as "dirty snowballs." The structure of a comet includes three parts. The **core,** or **nucleus,** is made up of frozen water and gases mixed with pieces of rocks and metal. The halo, called the **coma,** is a cloud of gas that surrounds the nucleus. Extending out from the coma is one or more **tails**. As the comet moves closer to the sun, the ice thaws and turns to vapor. This forms the coma of a comet. The nucleus and the coma form what is called the head of a comet. The comet's tail, a cloud of gas and dust, appears as a streak of light that points away from the sun.

How Comets Form

Comets are believed to be formed from the **Oort cloud**, a vast, moving mass of icy cosmic debris that lies beyond the orbit of Pluto. Gravity from a passing star causes a chunk of icy rock to break free. The force propels the comet toward the inner regions of our solar system. As it approaches the sun, the ice within it vaporizes and forms the glow. Very bright comets can be seen without a telescope. Comets travel in long **ellipses**, or deep orbits, around the sun. For most of their trip around the sun, they are invisible. Comets were formed billions of years ago when the solar system was young.

Long-Distance Travelers

Most comets take many years to complete a single orbit called a **period**. Short-orbit comets complete their orbits in less than two hundred years. These comets move within the area in which the planets are located. Other comets have huge, deep orbits that may take millions of years to complete. With each solar trip, a comet loses some of its material because the nucleus is being vaporized. Over time, it appears less bright, and all that is left are small particles. These small particles, which are spread throughout the comet's orbit, combine with particles from other sources and form **meteoroids**.

Famous Comets

The most famous short-orbit comet is Halley's comet. Halley's comet appears every 75 to 76 years. Its most recent arrival was in 1986, and it is expected to return in 2061. NASA is planning a future mission called Comet Rendezvous and Asteroid Flyby (CRAF). The mission may include flying with a comet's nucleus for a period of time, and a lander may set down on the comet's nucleus. Would you like to be a part of that future encounter?

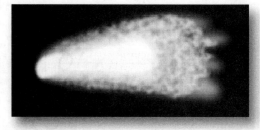

28

Name: _____ Date: _____

What Is a Comet?: Reinforcement Activity

To the student explorer: Can you explain what a comet is? _____

_____

Analyze: Why are comets sometimes called "dirty snowballs"? _____

_____

Directions: Complete the sentences below.

1. The three parts of a comet are the nucleus, the _____, and the
   _____.

2. Comets orbit the sun in long _____.

3. _____ comet orbits the sun every 75 to 76 years.

4. The _____ _____ is a moving mass of icy cosmic debris from which comets are thought to originate.

5. For most of their trip around the sun, comets are _____.

6. Comets get _____ each time they complete a solar trip.

7. The _____ of a comet is a cloud of gas and dust that appears as a streak of light.

8. The comet's _____ is made of frozen water, gas, and pieces of rocks and metals.

9. The _____ is a cloud of gas that surrounds the nucleus.

10. Comets formed _____ of years ago when the solar system was young.

11. Small pieces of an old comet's nucleus combine with other particles in space to form
    _____.

12. Ice and dust _____ as the comet comes near the sun.

Directions: Can you label the parts of the comet drawn below?

A. _____   B. _____   C. _____

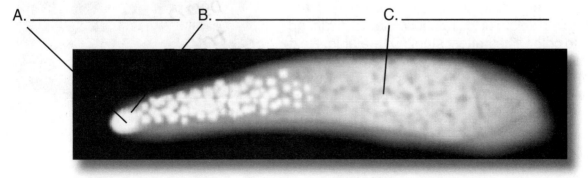

What Is a Star?

When you look up at the sky on a clear night, you see thousands of tiny points of light. These points of light are stars. A **star** is a big ball of gases that gives off heat and light. Stars can appear to be very tiny, dim white lights or very large, bright lights. Do you ever wonder why some stars appear brighter and larger than the others do? The way a star appears in the sky depends on its distance from Earth. The closer to Earth they are, the bigger they appear to be.

When you refer to the brightness of a star, you are referring to its **magnitude**. A star's magnitude may be absolute or apparent; **absolute magnitude** is how bright a star would appear to be at a set distance from Earth. **Apparent magnitude** is how bright the star appears when viewed from Earth. So what is the difference between absolute and apparent magnitude? Absolute is a measure of the amount of light given off by a star. Apparent is a measure of the amount of light received on Earth from a star.

Formation of Stars

A star is born from a cloud of gas and dust in space called a **nebula**. Gravity causes the nebula to contract and start to spin. After contracting and rotating for millions of years, the center of the cloud becomes hot. This flattens the nebula into a disk. Material at the center of the disk forms a protostar. A **protostar** is the material in the center of a nebula that is about to become a star. The temperature and pressure build, and nuclear reactions begin. Hydrogen atoms, the most common element in stars, smash together and create helium. During the reactions, the helium escapes, and the protostar gives off heat and light. A star is born!

Classification

Stars are classified in two different ways—according to **size** and **spectra** (colors). By size, stars are classified from largest to smallest. The largest and brightest stars are called **supergiants**. **Giants** make up the next largest group. **Main-sequence stars** are the third group; these are the average or medium-sized stars. **White dwarfs** are the next to the smallest group; these are small stars (about the size of Earth) that are slowly cooling. **Neutron stars** are the smallest group. Stars come in many colors, depending on their temperature or luminosity. The temperature and chemical composition of stars have an effect on the light produced. Scientists use a spectroscope to learn about the composition of each star, as well as its temperature. The spectroscope acts as a prism to spread the white light out into its patterns of color. White light contains red, orange, yellow, green, blue, indigo, and violet; these are the colors of the rainbow. Stars are ranked according to color. The hottest stars (O) are blue. Next are the white stars (B and A). Then there are the yellow stars (F and G). The cooler stars (K) are orange, while the coolest stars (M) tend to be redder in color.

What Is a Star? (cont.)

Star Patterns

Stars connected in a specific pattern (shape) against the dark sky form **constellations**. There are 88 constellations identified by astronomers. **Astronomy**, the study of stars, planets, and other objects in space, is the oldest science. Many of the constellations were named after animals and people of ancient Greek mythology. The locations of the constellations depend on the time of year, the time of night, and the location of the stargazer. The constellations visible in the Northern Hemisphere are different from those visible in the Southern Hemisphere. The stars are stationary; it is the movement of the earth that makes it look as if the stars are changing their positions.

One of the easiest constellations for young stargazers to find in the northern sky is Ursa Major; the name means "big bear." The Big Dipper is part of this pattern of stars. The Big Dipper is made up of seven stars, three in the handle and four in the cup. The two bright stars in the cup are called pointers. They point to the North Star, Polaris. Polaris is the first star in the handle of the Little Dipper. The Little Dipper is in Ursa Minor (the "little bear"), another constellation in the northern sky. To find constellations, go out on a dark night and search the sky. Use sky charts and look for the brightest stars first. Orion, the hunter, is one of the easiest patterns to find in the winter sky. It can be seen from both the Northern and Southern Hemispheres. Look for three bright stars on Orion's belt; Betelgeuse is one of them. Rigel, another bright star in this pattern, is on his knee.

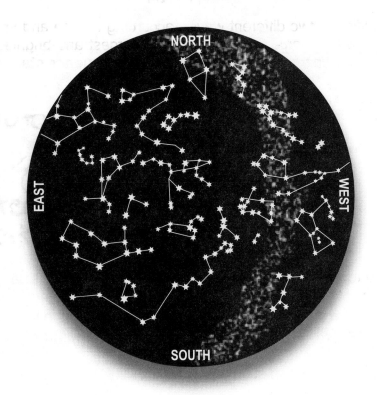

Name: _____ Date: _____

What Is a Star?: Reinforcement Activity

To the student explorer: Can you explain what a star is? _____

_____

_____

Analyze: Based on what you have learned about stars, which star is the closest one to Earth?

_____

Directions: Complete the following sentences.

1. A star is born from a cloud of gas called a _____.

2. _____ and _____ are the two gases that make up most stars.

3. _____ refers to the brightness of a star.

4. A star's _____ magnitude measures the amount of light given off by the star.

5. A star's _____ magnitude measures the amount of light received on Earth.

6. _____ stars are the hottest stars.

7. _____ stars are the coolest stars.

8. Scientists use _____ to learn about the properties of the star.

9. _____ light contains seven colors.

Directions: Using your own paper, see if you can answer the questions below.

10. Can you explain how a star is born or formed? Be sure to use the following words in your explanation: **nebula, gravity, spin, center, temperature, reaction.**

11. What are the two ways in which stars are classified?

What Is a Galaxy?

Gravity Groups

A **galaxy** is a huge collection of stars, gas, and dust that travels together through space. Galaxies are the building blocks of the universe. This huge group is held together by gravity. Galaxies are considered large when they contain over a trillion stars and small if they contain a billion stars or less. Beyond our galaxy, separated by vast tracts of empty space, lie billions of other galaxies.

Scientists have **classified** (grouped) the galaxies according to three basic shapes. Some galaxies have a rounded, elliptical shape. These galaxies are large, three-dimensional, and very common; they are known as the **elliptical** galaxies and resemble a slightly flattened ball. The stars in these galaxies are red and older than the stars in other galaxies. A second type of galaxy is the **spiral** galaxy. Spiral galaxies are shaped like flattened disks. They usually have one or more spiral arms that branch out from their centers. When viewed from the top, a spiral galaxy looks like a pinwheel. Some have barred spirals with stars and gases in a central bar. The reason for the straight bar of these galaxies is not completely understood. It is thought to be due to an even balance of forces—between magnetic forces in the galaxy and the rotational forces. Stars in spiral galaxies are mainly blue. Our galaxy, the Milky Way, is an example of a normal spiral galaxy. A third type of galaxy is the **irregular** galaxy. These are smaller, less common, and fainter galaxies with no regular shape. The irregular galaxies do not fit into the other two groups. Irregular galaxies are the closest neighbors to our own galaxy, the Milky Way.

Spiral   **Elliptical**

Barred Spiral   **Irregular**

Our Galaxy: The Milky Way

Our home in space is the Milky Way galaxy. It is a medium-sized spiral galaxy containing about 100 billion stars. The Milky Way is a part of a galaxy cluster named the **local group**, a group of about thirty galaxies. It is the second-largest galaxy in our local group. The stars in our galaxy are not evenly distributed. On a dark night, you can see a faint band of light stretching across the sky. It appears milky to the naked eye; this is where it gets its name. However, when you view it through a pair of binoculars, the "milkyness" disappears, and a faint light can be seen to come from stars clustered closely together.

The Milky Way is a conglomeration of stars, gases, and dust 100,000 light-years across. A **light-year** is the distance that light travels in one year and is about 5,880,000,000,000 miles. This vast distance is very hard to visualize or comprehend, wouldn't you agree?

The Milky Way can be divided into three main parts. The **center** is a spherical bulge of closely packed stars. Radiating out from it are wispy **arms** of stars, gases, and dust that form a disk 100,000 light-years in diameter and 2,500 light-years thick. The third part of the galaxy is its **halo**, a more sparsely populated sphere of stars that is an extension of the central bulge. The sun is in a spiral arm about two-thirds of the way from the center of the Milky Way galaxy. The position of the Milky Way in the night sky as seen from Earth, on a clear moonless night, depends on the time of night and the season of the year. In the winter, it will be directly overhead during the early evening. In the summer, it will be lower, nearer the northern horizon.

The Milky Way rotates like a wheel, and the sun and all of its attendants are carried around it once every 200 million years. Our closest neighbors are the Magellanic Cloud and the Small Magellanic Cloud. These irregular galaxies are 160,000 and 200,000 light-years away.

The Milky Way Galaxy

Name: _____ Date: _____

What Is a Galaxy?: Reinforcement Activity

To the student explorer: Can you explain what a galaxy is? _____

_____

Analyze: What constitutes a "large" galaxy as opposed to a "small" one?

_____

_____

Directions: Complete the statements below.

1. Galaxies are made up of billions of _____.

2. Galaxies are classified according to their _____.

3. There are three main types of _____.

4. Our home in space is the _____ _____

   galaxy.

5. A(n) _____ galaxy looks like a pinwheel with arms that branch

   from the center.

6. A(n) _____ galaxy resembles a slightly flattened ball.

7. A(n) _____ galaxy has no regular shape.

8. The Milky Way is a _____ galaxy.

9. The Milky Way is a part of a galaxy cluster named the _____ group.

10. The Milky Way galaxy is about _____ light-years across.

Directions: List the three main parts of our galaxy according to the descriptions below.

11. _____ – spherical bulge of closely packed stars

12. _____ – wispy extensions of stars, gases, and dust

13. _____ – sparsely populated sphere of stars that is an extension

    of the central bulge

35

Black Holes—Mysterious Objects in the Cosmos

Black holes have been around since the beginning of time. We didn't know about them until astronomers started exploring space with radio waves, x-rays, and infrared, ultraviolet, and gamma rays. Invisible radiation has brought information to us about unknown and mysterious objects in space that we call **black holes**. A black hole starts out as a massive, brilliant star. It is created by the explosion or collapse of the massive star—a **super nova**. Black holes come in many sizes and are often found at the centers of galaxies. It is a place where an object is so dense and the gravitational field surrounding it is so strong that not even light can escape its pull. That is how a black hole gets its name; the absence of light is what we see. It is also believed that when black holes gobble up stars and planets into their mass, the movement of the particles is like pouring water down a drain, creating a vortex, or swirling pattern. Simply put, a black hole can form when a massive star collapses in on itself. It is so dense that nothing pulled into it by gravity can come out. So how have we identified something we can't see?

Evidence

One explanation is something called an event horizon. Scientists have detected radiation coming from empty black spaces in the universe. They have hypothesized that this is a result of two particles coming very close together and causing an energy exchange. One particle becomes negatively charged, and the other particle becomes positively charged. They believe that the negative particle is pulled into the hole first, and in a flash, the positive particle is shot away from the negative and escapes out into space. This constant shooting out of high-energy particles creates radiation, suggesting the existence of a black hole.

Formation

In massive stars, fusion causes higher temperatures and greater expansion. The star expands into a **supergiant**. The core crashes inward, causing the outer part to explode. Because of the tremendous mass and strong gravitational pull, the matter at the center of the black hole is squeezed into an infinitely tiny point. When matter falls into these massive black holes, the bursts of light and energy released are called **quasars**. Quasars glow brighter than the light of thousands of galaxies. Some scientists believe that the birth of a black hole and its surrounding quasar is a by-product of the birth of a galaxy.

36

Name: _____ Date: _____

Solar System: Research Project

To the student explorer: Select a research topic from the list below or develop a topic of your own with the help of your teacher. Once you have decided on a topic that interests you, you will need to gather information about it. Your research must include three to five resources about your topic. Follow your teacher's directions for the format and length of your presentation. Your teacher will supply you in advance with a rubric or set of criteria for your project to let you know how your project will be judged. Let's go exploring!

Topic Suggestions:

- Did an asteroid striking the earth cause the extinction of the dinosaurs?

- Do black holes in space really exist?

- How can we tell how far away a star is?

- How do the inner planets compare and contrast with the outer planets?

- Is there a tenth planet?

- How far has the study of our solar system come? (history)

- What likely caused the craters on the surfaces of planets and moons?

- How and when did the universe begin?

- How does the sun make life on Earth possible?

- Could life exist on any of the other planets?

- How do telescopes detect electromagnetic waves in space?

- How does a rocket work?

- How are satellites, space shuttles, and space probes used to explore space?

© Mark Twain Media, Inc., Publishers   37

Name: _____ Date: _____

Solar System: Research Project Rubric

Solar System Project Requirements:

	Level 3: Advanced	Level 2: Proficient	Level 1: Basic	Level 0: No Attempt
Organization of Research Paper	• Clear expression of topic • Systematic organization of ideas	• Mostly clear expression of topic • Mostly systematic organization of ideas	• Somewhat clear expression of topic • No systematic organization of ideas	• Little or no attempt made to follow project guidelines
Major Findings	• Topic well developed • Clear expression of major findings	• Topic mostly developed • Mostly clear expression of major findings	• Topic not clearly developed • Some expression of major findings	• Little or no attempt made to follow project guidelines
Data Table/Graph	• Contains a data table or graph that is accurate and detailed	• Contains a data table or graph that is mostly accurate and detailed	• Contains a data table or graph that has limited accuracy and detail	• Little or no attempt made to follow project guidelines
Conclusion/ Recommendation	• Correct conclusion based on findings • Supports conclusion with detail	• Correct conclusion based on findings but may not state clearly • Supports conclusion with some detail	• Conclusion is incorrect or unclear • Support is missing or incorrect	• Little or no attempt made to follow project guidelines
Bibliography/ Sources	• At least 5 sources: 1 encyclopedia only 2 or more Internet 2 or more books and/or magazines • Citations are in correct format	• At least 3 sources: 1 encyclopedia only 1 or more Internet 1 or more books and/or magazines • Citations are mostly correct	• Sources are missing or not from 3 areas: 1 encyclopedia only 1 or more Internet 1 or more books and/or magazines • Citations are mostly incorrect and missing	• Little or no attempt made to follow project guidelines

Scoring criteria: Level 3 = 3 points; Level 2 = 2 points; Level 1 = 1 point; Level 0 = 0 points

Exceeds: 12–15 points; **Meets:** 8–11 points; **Does not meet:** 0–7 points

Total points earned by student: _____

Name: _____ Date: _____

Solar System: Vocabulary Study Sheet

To the student explorer: This is a list of important terms from the unit. Use the terms and their definitions to help you complete the activities in this unit. This study sheet will help you to prepare for the unit test.

1. **Absolute magnitude** - measure of the amount of light a star actually gives off
2. **Apparent magnitude** - measure of the amount of a star's light received on Earth
3. **Asteroids** - pieces of rock and metal similar to that which formed planets
4. **Asteroid Belt** - a region between Mars and Jupiter where most asteroids are found
5. **Atmosphere** - envelope of gases that surrounds Earth
6. **Axis** - an imaginary line through the center of a planet around which that body spins
7. **Black hole** - a massive star that has collapsed in on itself and whose gravity is so powerful that it pulls everything in, even light
8. **Comet** - a lump of ice, rock, frozen gas, and dust that orbits the sun
9. **Constellation** - a group of stars that forms a pattern in the sky
10. **Galaxy** - a group of stars, gases, and dust held together by gravity and that travels through space
11. **Light-year** - used to measure distance in space; equal to the distance that light travels in one year
12. **Meteor** - a small meteoroid that burns up in Earth's atmosphere
13. **Meteorite** - a meteoroid that strikes the earth
14. **Meteoroid** - small pieces of comet that move through space
15. **Milky Way** - a spiral galaxy; our home in space (Earth's galaxy)
16. **Nebula** - a cloud of gas and dust in space that forms stars
17. **Orbit** - the curved path of a satellite around another body in space
18. **Quasar** - a burst of bright light and energy from a black hole that has pulled in matter
19. **Rotation** - the spinning of a planet or another body on its axis
20. **Solar eclipse** - occurs when the moon passes between the earth and the sun
21. **Star** - a ball of gases that gives off light and heat
22. **Sun** - a yellow, average, middle-aged star

23. **Sunspots** - dark areas on the sun cooler than their surroundings
24. **Waning phases** - the phases of the moon that occur after the full moon as the visible side of the moon grows smaller, or decreases
25. **Waxing phases** - the phases of the moon after the new moon as the visible side of the moon grows larger, or increases

Name: _____ Date: _____

Solar System: Word Search

To the student explorer: In the word search puzzle, find and circle the solar system words listed below. Words are printed forward, backward, horizontally, vertically, and diagonally.

```
G X P B O U T E R P L A N E T S G W N B M G D F
P Z L B W K I C O N S T E L L A T I O N S N R G
I J U M S A I W Y D E X Z O G C F K U Y M J N S
S X T E A Q V J U Z A E M E T T B W O C Q Y T F
R E O R T T L E B D I O R E T S A Y V Y L O P L
R B U C U S Y I I E Y Q H N K M D E Q I P Q Y W
Q G L U R O Y E Q W M K H Q T F N V G S R H R Q
Z Z U R N R K A R U I Y M I P U Y H N S Z N Y V
V Z R Y F D S R U W D X D J S I T U C R A H D F
S R X Z I V O T J U L A N A N Y S A L A C S I A
G W R U J S J H Y P H L H M E O V C G M U P C A
N B J Y Z H E A C Q G A Z A Q N W N T N S A L W
Z E S Y A D W L R L E G R N N J O L A X R I X J
X Z B R H Y O B O F Y F P F D X T R Z V O D A V
I I U U K E J Q B H Z R I U Q N U D T R E T L J
F R F L L U G R C G K B D Q O J Y F S N T U F X
C Q I C P A R Q M J W C U J U P I T E R E N N X
N M B O G P M O O N P H A S E S S C L D M Y N R
E A B D L R N W A M H R E L T I B R O T Y M G W
P W S T E N A L P R E N N I B B Z M A U W Q D O
T L Z N U K I B B O G O D W W W P C L S F P W P
U C R K Y B L N C O M E T S Q I K I H W A N I N
N L A N U X G O R M Y N D B Q D G R H A R U M X
E X Z N C P S P M E T S Y S R A L O S Z W K Q K
```

Asteroid Belt	black holes	comets	constellations
Earth	galaxy	inner planets	Jupiter
light-year	Mars	Mercury	meteors
Milky Way	moon phases	nebula	Neptune
orbit	outer planets	Pluto	quasars
Saturn	solar system	sunspots	Uranus
Venus			

Name: _____ Date: _____

Solar System: Crossword Puzzle

To the student explorer: Complete the puzzle with the information you have learned in this unit.

ACROSS

3. A cloud of dust and gas that becomes a star
5. Our home in space
7. The largest planet
9. Groups of stars that form patterns in the sky
16. Jupiter, Saturn, Uranus, Neptune, Pluto (two words)
17. The planet closest to the sun
18. Massive star that has collapsed and pulls everthing in, even light (two words)
20. The sixth planet from the sun
23. A group of stars, gases, and dust held together by gravity and that travels through space
24. The second planet from the sun
25. Dark area on the sun that is cooler than its surroundings

DOWN

1. The smallest and most distant planet
2. A lump of ice, rock, frozen gas, and dust that orbits the sun
4. Nicknamed the "red planet"
6. The center of our solar system
8. Mercury, Venus, Earth, and Mars (two words)
10. Usually the eighth planet from the sun
11. The planet on which we live
12. Between Mars and Jupiter, where most asteroids are found (two words)
13. A ball of gases that gives off light and heat
14. A burst of brilliant light from a black hole
15. The seventh planet from the sun
19. Curved path of a satellite around another body in space
21. Used to measure distance in space; equal to the distance light travels in one year
22. A small meteoroid that burns up in Earth's atmosphere

Name: _____ Date: _____

Solar System: Unit Test

I. **Directions:** Match each term in the first column with its definition in the second column. Write the letter of the correct definition in the blank at the left.

_____ 1. Galaxies

_____ 2. Nebula

_____ 3. Constellations

_____ 4. Solar System

_____ 5. Satellite(s)

_____ 6. Sun

_____ 7. Meteors

_____ 8. Asteroid Belt

_____ 9. Light-year

_____ 10. Orbit

_____ 11. Atmosphere

_____ 12. Comet

A. A cloud of gas and dust in space that forms stars

B. Lump of ice, rock, frozen gas, and dust that orbits the sun and has a tail

C. Moon(s) orbiting a body in space

D. The sun and all of the objects that orbit it

E. The center of our solar system

F. Movement of one object in a curved path around another

G. Unit to measure distances between objects in space

H. The air that surrounds the earth

I. Separates the inner and outer planets

J. Space objects that burn up as they enter Earth's atmosphere

K. Patterns of stars against the night sky

L. Huge collections of stars, gas, and dust traveling through space

II. **Multiple Choice:** Write the letter of the correct answer on the line at the left.

_____ 13. The planet closest in size to Earth is
    A. Venus.   B. Mercury.   C. Pluto.   D. Jupiter.

_____ 14. The Great Red Spot is a well-known feature of
    A. Neptune.   B. Jupiter.   C. Pluto.   D. Uranus.

_____ 15. The only star close enough for us to study is
    A. the sun.   B. the moon.   C. Venus.   D. Neptune.

_____ 16. The planet that is closest to the sun is
    A. Earth.   B. Mars.   C. Mercury.   D. Pluto.

_____ 17. The only two planets without a moon are
    A. Venus and Earth.   B. Jupiter and Pluto.
    C. Jupiter and Mercury.   D. Venus and Mercury.

_____ 18. The four seasons on Earth are caused by
    A. the tilt of the earth.   B. Earth's rotation.
    C. Earth's atmosphere.   D. heat currents.

Name: _____ Date: _____

Solar System: Unit Test (cont.)

_____ 19. The dark features of the moon are called
     A. oceans.   B. maria.   C. waning.   D. highlands.

_____ 20. The visible part of the moon increases as the moon is
     A. waning.   B. waxing.   C. crescenting.   D. expanding.

_____ 21. The red planet is
     A. Pluto.   B. Venus.   C. Mars.   D. Mercury.

_____ 22. The minor planets are
     A. meteors.   B. meteoroids.   C. asteroids.   D. comets.

_____ 23. "Dirty snowballs" with long, elliptical orbits are
     A. meteors.   B. meteoroids.   C. asteroids.   D. comets.

_____ 24. A massive star that has collapsed and pulls everything in, even light, is a(n)
     A. comet.   B. black hole.   C. planet.   D. asteroid.

_____ 25. The largest planet is
     A. Earth.   B. Jupiter.   C. Pluto.   D. Venus.

_____ 26. The smallest planet is
     A. Earth.   B. Jupiter.   C. Pluto.   D. Venus.

_____ 27. All of the following are outer planets except
     A. Earth.   B. Jupiter.   C. Saturn.   D. Uranus.

_____ 28. The Great Red Spot is actually a(n)
     A. ocean.   B. storm.   C. moon.   D. crater.

_____ 29. Several rings are the main features of the planet
     A. Jupiter.   B. Uranus.   C. Mars.   D. Saturn.

_____ 30. Our galaxy is the
     A. Elliptical galaxy.   B. Halley's galaxy.
     C. Earth galaxy.   D. Milky Way galaxy.

Answer Keys

What Is the Solar System?: Reinforcement Activity (p. 3)
To the student observer: Nine known planets: Mercury, Venus, Earth, Mars, Jupiter, Saturn, Uranus, Neptune, Pluto
Analyze: Because they seemed to change their locations in the sky.
1. A nebula is a spinning cloud of gas and dust in space. One may have formed our solar system.
2. The inner planets are Mercury, Venus, Earth, and Mars.
3. The outer planets are Jupiter, Saturn, Uranus, Neptune, and Pluto.
4. They are different in size and composition. The inner planets are small and made of rock. The outer planets are large and gaseous except for Pluto.
5. asteroid belt   6. nebula   7. orbit
8. center   9. light-year
10. asteroids, comets

What Is the Sun?: Reinforcement Activity (p. 5)
To the student observer: The sun is an average star in size, mass, and temperature.
Analyze: It's closer to the earth than any of the other stars.
1. layers of burning gas
2. the core and the atmosphere
3. the core
4. photosphere, chromosphere, and the corona
5. chromosphere and corona
6. **A**tmosphere   7. **S**un   8. **P**lanets
9. **E**clipse   10. **C**ore   11. **I**n
12. **A**toms   13. **L**argest
14. **S**unspots   15. **T**hree   16. **A**verage
17. **R**eactions

Mercury, Extreme Desolation: Reinforcement Activity (p. 7)
To the student observer: the inner planets and the outer planets
Analyze: Mercury is at an almost 0-degree tilt on its axis; therefore, it revolves around the sun almost perfectly straight up and down.
1. The inner planets are Mercury, Venus, Earth, and Mars.
2. They are small, dense (heavy), rocky planets with a core of molten iron. All four of the inner planets are closer to the sun than the outer planets.
3. The lack of water and atmosphere to hold in the heat makes it impossible for life to exist on Mercury. The temperatures are too extreme.
4. The surface of Mercury is about the same size and has a similar surface as our moon. It has many craters.
5. **M**ercury   6. **E**xtreme   7. **R**ocky
8. **C**entral core   9. **U**nmanned   10. **R**adar
11. **Y**ear on Mercury

Venus, the Hostile Furnace: Reinforcement Activity (p. 9)
To the student observer: Mercury and Earth
Analyze: It is similar to Earth in size, mass, and density.
1. high temperatures, non-breathable air (carbon dioxide), and a crushing atmospheric pressure
2. Thick clouds surround the planet and reflect the sun's light.
3. carbon dioxide

4. They were crushed by the atmospheric pressure (90 times that of Earth's).
5. The surface is oceanless with rolling plains, highland plateaus, mountains, valleys, craters, and active volcanoes.
6. **V**enus   7. **E**vening   8. **N**atural
9. **U**nlike   10. **S**econd

Earth, the Planet on Which We Live: Reinforcement Activity (p. 11)
To the student observer: favorable temperatures and a suitable atmosphere
Analyze: The earth is 70 percent water. The oceans give Earth its blue color.
1. Earth rotates on its axis approximately every 24 hours.
2. Nitrogen is the most abundant gas in our atmosphere.
3. The moon is airless, lifeless, and has no active volcanoes.
4. A. Earth's crust   B. mantle
   C. outer core   D. inner core
5. **E**arth   6. **A**tmosphere   7. **R**otates
8. **T**ilt   9. **H**eat

What Is Earth's Natural Satellite?: Reinforcement Activity (p. 14)
To the student observer: The moon has less mass than Earth; therefore, its gravitational pull is less than Earth's. (You should be able to jump six times higher on the moon, due to less gravity.)
Analyze: The moon has no atmosphere and extreme temperatures, ranging from 100°C to -160°C.
1. rotates   2. sun   3. sunlight
4. Neil Armstrong 5. maria   6. mountains
7. shape   8. waxing   10. waning

Phases of the Moon Activity (p. 15)

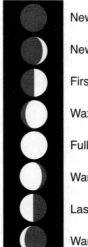

New Moon
New or Waxing Crescent
First Quarter
Waxing Gibbous
Full Moon
Waning Gibbous
Last Quarter
Waning Crescent

Mars, the Red Dust Bowl Planet: Reinforcement Activity (p. 17)
To the student observer: Yes, it has a reddish surface color, and it is a very dry planet with high winds.
Analyze: Mars is close to Earth, and it is not hidden by the glare of the sun or covered up by thick clouds.
1. It might be frozen beneath the surface, since it can get so cold, or it may have evaporated into the atmosphere. Accept any logical answer here.

44

2. Earth and Mars have similar seasons, air pressure, and length of day.
3. Not as we live on Earth. We need to get more oxygen on the planet because we couldn't breathe there. Water would be another problem; we would need to find a way to get and use water. Accept any logical problem-solving answer that students provide. (Plants for oxygen, heat source for extremely cold seasons, special suits for living in a manmade biosphere with all of our needs)
4. Locked in rocks or frozen in the polar ice caps
5. **M**ars   6. **A**ntarctica   7. **R**ed
8. **S**urface

What Are Minor Planets?: Reinforcement Activity (p. 19)
To the student observer: Between Mars and Jupiter
Analyze: Because they are smaller than planets, and they orbit the sun as planets do.
1. debris, or chunks of rock and metals, that orbit the sun
2. in the asteroid belt, a 300-million-mile gap between Mars and Jupiter
3. small pieces of asteroids and other objects in space (rocks and dust) that break off
4. Meteors are metoroids that enter Earth's atmosphere and create a streak of bright light.
5. No, a shooting star isn't a star; it is a meteor that moves across the night sky.
6. Sporadic meteors are meteors that can occur at any time. Meteor showers occur at predictable points in Earth's orbit.
7. It's a larger meteoroid that actually reaches the Earth's surface.
8. Meteoroids burn up upon entering Earth's atmosphere from the heat and friction.

Jupiter, the Gas Giant: Reinforcement Activity (p. 21)
To the student observer: Jupiter is a cold, giant, gaseous planet with 16 moons and two faint rings.
Analyze: Yes, Jupiter was named after the king of the gods. It is the largest planet, which makes it the king of planets.
1. The Great Red Spot is a huge storm similar to a cyclone. Steam and ammonia rising from the atmosphere is the cause.
2. hydrogen and helium
3. Jupiter rotates in ten hours, compared to Earth's 24 hours. (This makes Jupiter's spin almost $2\frac{1}{2}$ times faster than that of Earth's.) However, it revolves around the sun 12 times slower than Earth.
4. **J**upiter   5. **U**ranus   6. **P**lanet
7. **I**nclude   8. **T**elescope   9. **E**arth
10. **R**apid

Saturn, the Ringed Planet: Reinforcement Activity (p. 23)
To the student observer: Saturn is the second-largest gas planet with several rings and many moons orbiting it.
Analyze: Saturn and Jupiter have a similar atmosphere of hydrogen and helium; they are both outer planets; both are giant gas planets; both have rings. Answers may vary somewhat; accept all logical answers.
1. Low density—it is less dense than water
2. Saturn's ring system consists of thin ringlets that orbit within several main rings. The rings are made of ice, rocks, and dust.

3. The thick clouds make the surface difficult for scientists to see.
4. **S**ixth   5. **A**nother   6. **T**wice
7. **U**se   8. **R**ings   9. **N**umber

Uranus and Neptune, the Pulling Planets: Reinforcement Activity (p. 25)
To the student observer: Possible answers: blue-green atmosphere, outer planets, rings, discovered much later (after the invention of the telescope)
Analyze: Its tilt on its axis (horizontal), it appears to be lying on its side.
1. Another unknown planet must exist. (Gravitational pull from another planet pulls it off course.)
2. that an actively changing atmosphere exists
3. **U**ranus   4. **R**inged   5. **A**xis
6. **N**ot   7. **U**nusual   8. **S**trong
9. **N**amed   10. **E**ight   11. **P**redicted
12. **T**elescope   13. **U**ranus   14. **N**eptune
15. **E**ight

Pluto, the Ninth and Smallest Planet: Reinforcement Activity (p. 27)
To the student observer: The planet of Pluto is the smallest, coldest, and the most distant (ninth) planet. Pluto's orbit is lopsided and steeply tilted.
Analyze: The tilt of the planet's orbit sometimes brings it closer to the sun than Neptune.
Interview Activity: Questions will vary. Students should address *who, what, when, where,* and *why.*
6. **P**luto   7. **L**ight   8. **U**ndiscovered
9. **T**ilted   10. **O**rbit

What Is a Comet?: Reinforcement Activity (p. 29)
To the student observer: A comet is a lump of ice, rock, frozen gas, and dust that orbits the sun.
Analyze: Accept any logical answer. Because a snowball is packed into frozen ice, and sometimes other things get mixed into the snowball, such as rock, grass, and dust, it can have a dirty appearance. When you throw a snowball, it can move through the air much as a comet moves through space.
1. coma, tail   2. ellipses
3. Halley's   4. Oort cloud
5. invisible   6. smaller
7. tail   8. core or nucleus
9. coma   10. billions
11. meteoroids   12. thaw or vaporize
Labeling Activity:
A. core or nucleus   B. coma   C. tail

What Is a Star?: Reinforcement Activity (p. 32)
To the student observer: A star is a hot, glowing ball of gases that gives off heat and light.
Analyze: The sun is the closest star to the earth.
1. nebula
2. Hydrogen, helium
3. Magnitude
4. absolute
5. apparent
6. Blue
7. Red
8. spectroscopes
9. White

10. Gravity causes the nebula to contract and spin. This causes the center of the nebula to become hot and flatten. Temperature and pressure builds, nuclear reactions occur, and heat and light are given off. (Answers may vary.)

11. Stars are classified by their size and spectra (colors).

What Is a Galaxy?: Reinforcement Activity (p. 35)
To the student observer: A galaxy is a large collection of stars, gas, and dust that travels together through space.
Analyze: A galaxy is considered large when it contains over a trillion stars and small if it contains a billion stars or less.

1. stars
2. shape
3. galaxies
4. Milky Way
5. spiral
6. elliptical
7. irregular
8. spiral
9. local
10. 100,000
11. center
12. arms
13. halo

Solar System: Crossword Puzzle (p. 41)

Solar System: Unit Test (p. 42–43)

1. L	2. A	3. K	4. D
5. C	6. E	7. J	8. I
9. G	10. F	11. H	12. B
13. A	14. B	15. A	16. C
17. D	18. A	19. B	20. B
21. C	22. C	23. D	24. B
25. B	26. C	27. A	28. B
29. D	30. D		

Solar System: Word Search (p. 40)

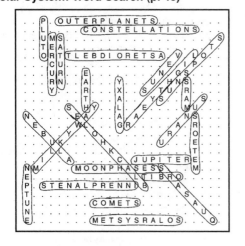

Bibliography

Bernstein, Schachter, Winkler, and Wolfe. *Concepts and Challenges, Earth Science.* Globe Fearon, 2003.

Coüper, Heather. *Space Scientist—The Planets.* Franklin Watts, 1985.

Couper, Heather and Henbest, Nigel. *Astronomy: Planets, Stars, and the Cosmos.* Franklin Watts, 1983.

Couper, Heather and Henbest, Nigel. *Black Holes: A Journey to the Heart of a Black Hole.* DK Publishing, 1996.

Feather, Snyder, and Zike. *Earth Science.* Glencoe/McGraw-Hill, 2002.

Jones, Brian and Gutelle, Andrew. *Our Solar System.* SMITHMARK Publishers, 1992.